Beginner Cello Method

Author: Carla Louro

Music recording and production: Carla Louro and Cátia Louro

Published by Arts2Science

Copyright © 2012 Arts2Science

http://www.arts2science.com

info@arts2science.com

All rights reserved.

ISBN-13: 978-989-97627-0-1

About the book

This book is a cello method for beginners and is composed of different chapters. The concepts and techniques are learned very progressively and are introduced by theory boxes and exercises. The pieces become progressively bigger and harder and are ordered by key signature and hand position. The songs in the book are well known classical themes from famous composers, popular folk tunes from several countries and pieces by the author. This book pays particular attention to rhythm, including exercises and pieces that will help you study rhythm. Playing the rhythm of a piece accurately is very important, especially because a cellist usually plays with other people (with piano accompaniment, a string quartet, an orchestra and in many other situations). You also have several scales and arpeggios to practice, because playing them is essential to master the different positions, different key signatures and achieve a good intonation. You can download the sound files that accompany the book at the http://www.arts2science.com website and play some exercises and pieces with an accompaniment. The sound files are located in a folder with the name of this book. For the pieces with piano accompaniment, you have two types of sound files: one with cello and piano and another with the piano part, so you can play along with the cello part. The numbers that appear in the scores are the numbers of the mp3 files. In this folder, you will also find rhythm accompaniments for the rhythm exercises, additional piano accompaniments that you won't find in this book and interactive applications about the cello. The website will be frequently updated with new material and recordings related to this book. This book teaches the first position, including extensions.

You will find symbols throughout the book that will tell you what you will be doing, or that you should pay attention to an important concept. These symbols are:

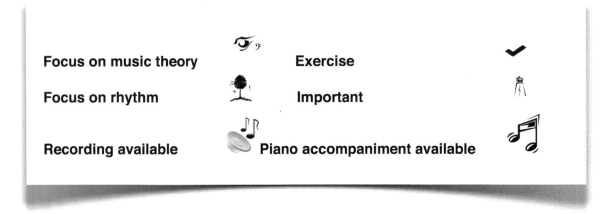

CONTENTS

1. Introduction to the cello — 6
- History of the cello — 7
- Parts of the cello — 8
- The Bow — 12
- Finger numbers — 13
- Parts of the bow — 16
- Terms and abbreviations — 18
- Exercises — 19

2. The staff, the bass clef and the open strings — 20
- The music staff — 21
- The clefs: the treble clef and the bass clef — 21
- The open strings — 25
- Measures and bar lines — 27
- Note duration — 27
- Pizzicato — 29
- Piece: "Open Strings" — 31

3. The first position — 32
- C Major: first position — 33
- Cello duet: "Jingle Bells", christmas song — 35
- Cello duet: "Twinkle, twinkle little star", by Mozart — 36
- Staccato, legato — 37
- Management of the bow — 39
- Exercises for the left hand — 41
- Piece: "Ode to Joy", by Beethoven — 43
- Piece: "Old Macdonald had a farm", children song — 43
- Piece: "We wish you a merry christmas", christmas song — 44
- Piece: "Tristesse", Chopin — 44
- Scales, C Major scale — 45
- Half steps and whole steps — 47
- First Position, G Major — 50
- Key signature — 50
- Sharps — 50
- G Major scale — 51

- Exercises for the notes in G Major	52
- Piece: "Lightly Row", children song	53
- Piece: "Au clair de la lune", trad. french song	54
- Piece: "Eu tenho um pião", trad. portuguese song	54
- Arpeggios	55
-Note duration	56
- Piece: "London Bridge", trad. english song	57
- Piece: "Eine kleine nachtmuzik", Mozart	57
- Natural symbol, repeat bar	58
- Piece: "Happy birthday"	58
- Piece: "Go tell aunt Rhody"	58
- First position, D Major	59
- Cello duet: "New world symphony", Dvoràk	61
- Piece: "The first Noel", christmas song	62
- Round, piece: "Round Time"	63
- Time signatures	64
- First position, F Major	66
- Rests, triplets	67
- Piece: "Minuet 2", Bach	68
- Dotted quarter notes, management of the bow	69
- First position extensions, D minor	70
- Minor scales	70
- Piece: "Minor scale", by Carla louro	72
- Canon, piece: "Old Canon"	73
- First position extensions, G minor	74
- Dotted eighth notes	74
- Dynamics	75
- Piece: "Não se me dá que vindimem", trad. portuguese song	75
- Piece: "Wie komm ich denn zur Tur herein", by J. Brahms	75
- Cello duet: "Fifth Symphony", by Beethoven	76
- Tie, slur	77
- Piece: "Senhora do Almurtão", trad. portuguese song	78
- First position extensions, D Major	79
- D Major scale and arpeggio in two octaves	79
- Exercises for extensions in D Major	80
- Piece: "Mary had a little lamb", american folk song	80

- Piece: "Yankee Doodle", American song	81
- Piece: "Spring", from the four seasons, by Vivaldi	81
- First position extensions, A Major	82
- Exercises in A Major	83
- Piece: "William Tell", by Rossini	83
- Transposition: C Major to E Major	84
- Exercises for extensions in E Major	84
- Piece: "Morning Song", by Grieg	85
- Étude 1, by Dotzauer	86
- First position revision fingering charts	87
- Revision piece: "Scarborough Fair", trad. english song	88
4. Repertoire pieces and different music styles	**89**
- Duble stops, changing meter	90
- Music styles, Blues	91
- Exercises for Blues and double stops	91
- Piece: "Blues in G", by Carla Louro	92
- Piece: "Folk Song", by Carla Louro	94
- Scales and arpeggios in two octaves, first position	95
5. Piano Accompaniments	**97**
- Piano accompaniment "Ode to Joy", by Beethoven	97
- Piano accompaniment "We wish you a merry Christmas"	98
- Piano accompaniment "Eine kleine nachtmuzik"	99
- Piano accompaniment "Morning Song"	100
- Piano accompaniment "Senhora do Almurtão"	102
- Piano accompaniment "Folk Song"	106

1 Introduction to the Cello

The Scroll

Before you start playing the cello, you need to learn important things about this instrument. By doing this, the experience of learning how to play the cello will be more rewarding and will also be based on strong theoretical and technical foundations.

This chapter is an introduction to cello history, cello anatomy and playing position. You will learn the name of the different parts of the cello, the bow and accessories. You will also learn important symbols and abbreviations that you will see many times in scores.

The cello is part of the orchestra. The standard position of the cello section in the orchestra is on the left, in front of the double basses and opposite the first violin section.

This chapter ends with exercises to practice the topics that you have learned so far.

Down Bow   *Up Bow*

History of the Cello

The cello is a bowed string instrument. This means that it is played with a bow on a string. You can also play it by plucking the strings with your fingers. This technique is called **pizzicato**.

The cello is very similar to the violin, viola and double bass on the basic way of playing, the use of the bow and how the instrument is built.

The history of the cello and other string instruments in Europe starts in the 9th century a.C. with the lira. The lira was also a bowed instrument in the Byzantine Empire.

The modern cellos were developed to their final form by Stradivarius, in 1680. In the 18th century, the cello became much more popular than the instruments from the viola da gamba family, which were very popular until then.

In the beginning, the cellos were mainly used to add a bass to the string family in the orchestra, but since the concerts of Boccherini it became a solo instrument as well.

Today the cello is used in solo music and is also a member of the symphony orchestra.

WHAT IS PIZZ.?

PARTS OF THE CELLO

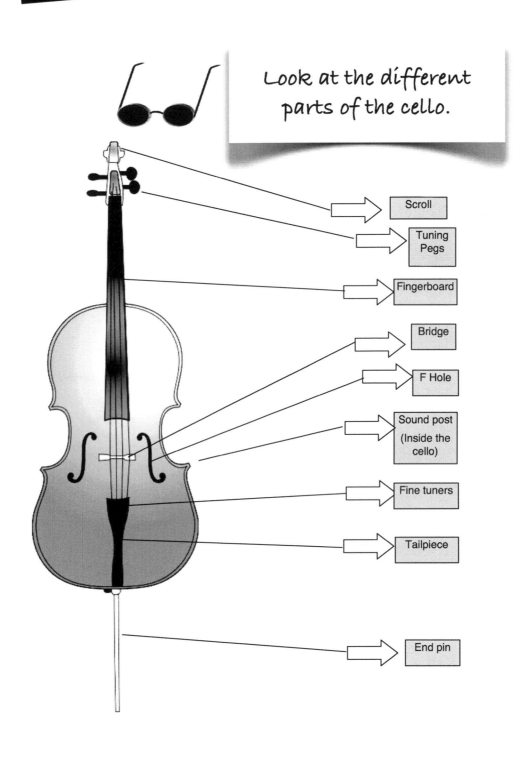

Look at the different parts of the cello.

- Scroll
- Tuning Pegs
- Fingerboard
- Bridge
- F Hole
- Sound post (Inside the cello)
- Fine tuners
- Tailpiece
- End pin

Learn the parts of the cello

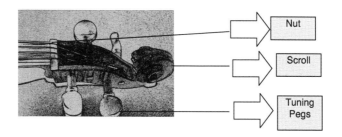

Cello parts and accessories

Strings

The cello has four strings. The first (I) is the A string, the second (II) is the D string, the third (III) is the G string and the fourth (IV) is the C string. They are numbered from the highest pitched string (I) to the lowest pitched string (IV).

Scroll

The scroll looks like a head at the top of the cello.

Fingerboard

The fingerboard is the black piece of wood where you put the fingers of your left hand. The four strings are over the fingerboard.

Bridge

The bridge is the piece of wood that holds the strings after the fingerboard.

F Holes

The two f holes are in fact holes shaped like an f. They are located on the left and right sides of the bridge.

CELLO PARTS AND ACCESSORIES

Tailpiece

The tailpiece is a small piece of wood on the bottom end of the cello which holds the strings and includes the fine tuners.

Fine Tuners

The fine tuners are four small screws in the tailpiece, which you use to tune each string of the cello. They are used when you don't have to lower or raise the string's pitch too much.

PARTS OF THE CELLO

Fine tuners

Homework

What's the difference between the tuning pegs and the fine tuners?

Tuning pegs

You can also use the tuning pegs to tune the cello, but when you have to lower or raise the string's pitch more. They are located on the cello's head, near the scroll and you have one for each string.

THE BOW

→ Tip
→ Hair
→ Frog
→ Tension screw

The **bow** is placed over the strings, between the fingerboard and the bridge. You hold it with your right hand and you should move it in a straight line.

? Name two parts of the bow.

Homework

Write down the names of these parts of the cello.

Finger numbers

When you play the cello, you use four fingers of your left hand.

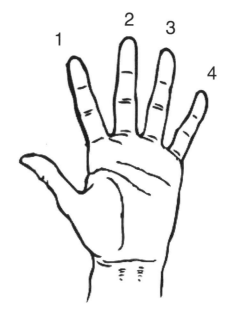

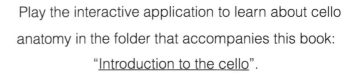
Play the interactive application to learn about cello anatomy in the folder that accompanies this book: "Introduction to the cello".

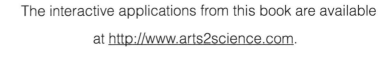
The interactive applications from this book are available at http://www.arts2science.com.

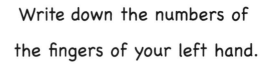
Write down the numbers of the fingers of your left hand.

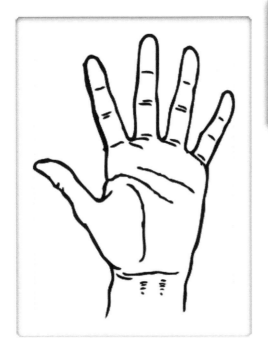

Important

When you use the bow, you have to tighten the hairs first. Then you rub the hairs with rosin. After you play, you have to loosen the hairs of the bow.

You play your bow up or down, according to the symbol that appears.

◫　**Down Bow**

V　**Up Bow**

 Exercises for playing with the bow.

Play with the bow on any string.

PARTS OF THE BOW

Tip

The tip is the narrow point of the bow, opposite to where you put your hand.

Frog

The frog is the part of the bow opposite the tip. You'll find it near the point where you place your right hand on the bow.

Stick

The stick is the wooden part of the bow. It is made of Pernambuco tree wood. Bows are also made of other materials, such as carbon-fibre (which is stronger than wood) and fiberglass (often used to make less expensive bows).

Adjusting screw

The adjusting screw is located near the frog and you use it to tighten or loosen the hair of the bow.

Hair

The hair is the part of the bow that touches the strings. Bows need to be re-haired periodically.

Rosin

The rosin is sticky. You rub it on the hair of the bow before you play. It causes friction so sound comes from the strings when you play with the bow over them.

IMPORTANT

How to sit down while playing

- The right way to sit down when you play the cello is by keeping your feet flat on the ground.

- The seat of the chair should be at the same level as your knee.

- You need to adjust the endpin, so you can have the cello at an appropriate height.

- The cello should rest against your chest. You should hold the cello between your knees. You should also sit down on the forward edge of the chair.

The left hand thumb finger

The left hand thumb finger should be under the second finger. When the second finger moves, the thumb should always follow.

Terms and abbreviations

Important

When you play the cello, you will find these terms and symbols many times. You should know all of them.

⊓	Down Bow	V	Up Bow
O	Harmonic	0	Open String
1	First Finger	2	Second Finger
3	Third Finger	4	Fourth Finger

| pizz. | play pizzicato (pluck the strings with the fingers of your right hand). |
| arco | Play with the bow (this word appears to tell you to play with the bow, when you were playing pizzicato before). |

I   This is the Roman numeral that tells you to play in the first string, the A String.

II   This is the Roman numeral that tells you to play in the second string, the D String.

III   This is the Roman numeral that tells you to play in the third string, the G String.

IV   This is the Roman numeral that tells you to play in the fourth string, the C String.

Ext.   Extension

Exercises about cello anatomy and symbols

Name the following parts of the cello.

What do these symbols and abbreviations mean?

IV _____   pizz _____

3 _____   V _____

arco _____   0 _____

II _____   ◻ _____

Describe the following parts of the cello and the bow. Try to identify them with your own cello.

Bridge _____

Tuning pegs _____

End pin _____

Fine tuners _____

Adjusting screw _____

Where are the cellos in the symphony orchestra? Choose the right answer.

A. Next to the Violins   B. Behind the Doubles Basses   C. In front of the Double Basses

2
The Staff, the Bass Clef and the Open Strings

The Bass Clef

Chapter 2 is an introduction to general music theory which is important to the cello player. You will learn about the music staff and the bass clef. It also introduces you to the open strings of the cello and other important topics.

This chapter includes several exercises to practice what you've learned.

Good Work

 ## Focus on Music Theory

The Music Staff

The notes are written in the Music Staff.

The staff has 5 lines and 4 spaces.

Lines   **Spaces**

The clefs: the treble clef and the bass clef

The Treble Clef

The "Clef" is what is used to assign specific note names to each of the lines and spaces. The "Treble Clef" and the "Bass Clef" are the most common clefs.

The treble clef tells us that the note G is in the second line.

Line 2

The note names in the Treble Clef are:

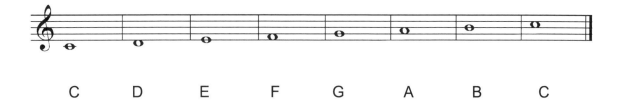

C   D   E   F   G   A   B   C

Play the interactive application about the bass clef in the folder that accompanies this book:

"The bass clef".

Complete this sentence:

The music staff has _____ lines and _____ spaces.

The Bass Clef

The Bass Clef tells us that the note F is in the fourth line.

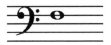 **Note F** Fourth Line

Important

The clef that you will use the most when you play the cello will be the bass clef.

The names of the notes in the bass clef are different from the ones in the treble clef.

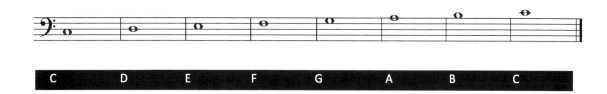

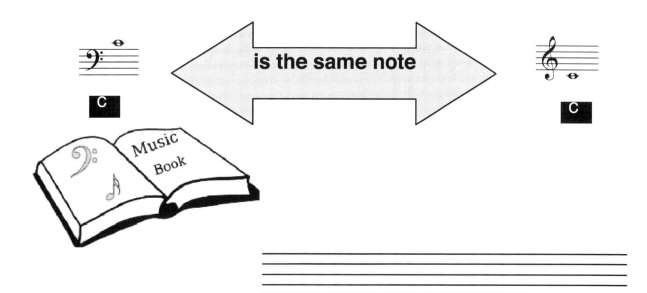

Use this staff to practice how to draw the bass clef. Remember to draw the two dots in the spaces around the fourth line.

Exercises about the bass clef

Write down the names of the following notes in the bass clef.

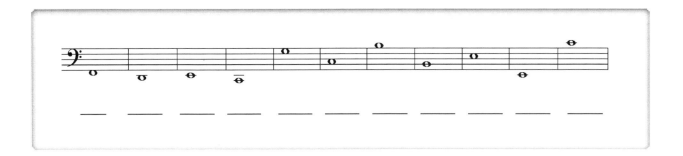

Answer the following questions:

- What's the name of the note in the second line in the bass clef? _____

- What's the name of the note in the fifth line in the bass clef? _____

- What's the name of the note in the second space in the bass clef? _____

- What's the name of the note in the fourth line in the bass clef? _____

- What's the name of the note in the third space in the bass clef? _____

The Open Strings

There are four open strings in the cello. These are the ones that you play without using the fingers of your left hand on the fingerboard.

Memorize the names of the strings, their number and how to write them on the bass clef.

String Name	C	G	D	A
String Number	IV	III	II	I

Use this staff to practice the four open strings of the cello on the bass clef. Write down their names.

String _____

Name _____

Listen to the open strings of the cello.
1. C String
2. G String
3. D String
4. A String

Play the interactive application to learn about the open strings in the folder that accompanies this book: "Introduction to the cello".

Exercises for the Open Strings

Use this staff to draw some notes in the bass clef and write down their names.

Play with the bow on the following open strings.

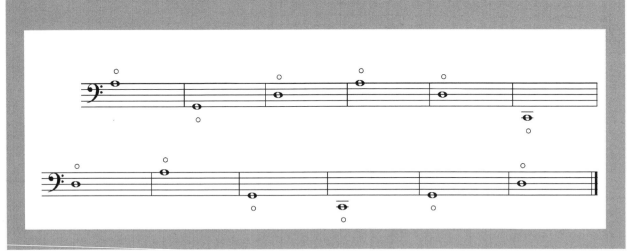

Name the open strings and write down their numbers. Then you can play the exercise.

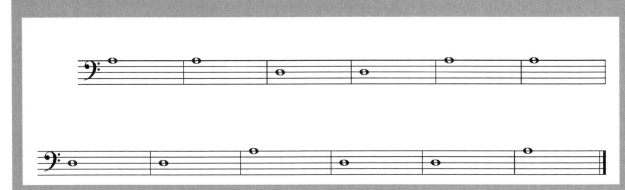

Focus on Music Theory

Measures and Bar lines

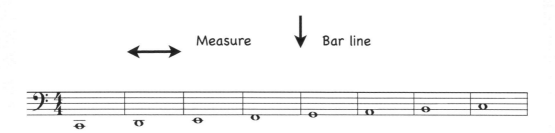

Focus on Rhythm

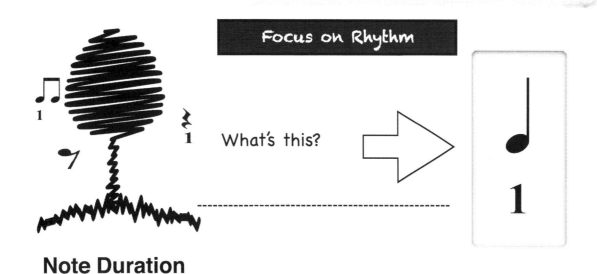

Note Duration

We speak of Note duration when we want to know how long we should play a note.

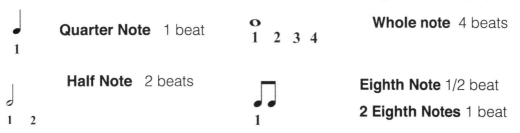

Rhythm exercises for the Open Strings

Play on the open strings.

Play on the open strings.

Improvisation: creativity with the open strings.

Now you will use your own imagination and play some open strings on the cello, listening to their sound. You can write down the notes that you played.

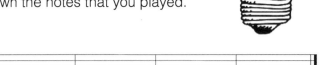

Name this part of the cello.

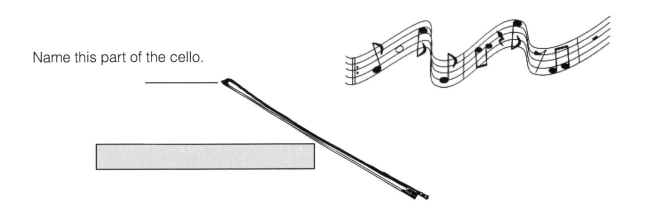

Exercise for pizzicato and music theory

Practice pizzicato with these exercises. Remember to play the notes with the right rhythm.

> **Pizzicato**
>
> Playing pizzicato is using your fingers to pluck the strings instead of using a bow. The word _pizz._ tells you to play pizzicato when it appears above the note. You play pizzicato all the time until the word _arco_ appears.

Practice pizzicato with this exercise on any string. Remember to play the notes with the right rhythm. You can use the metronome (slow or fast) in the folder that accompanies this book.

Now you will see the notes in the staff and you will write down which finger you will use to play them and their names.

Finger number: 0   2   __   __   __   __   __   __   __   __

Note name: A   C   __   __   __   __   __   __   __   __

What's this? _____

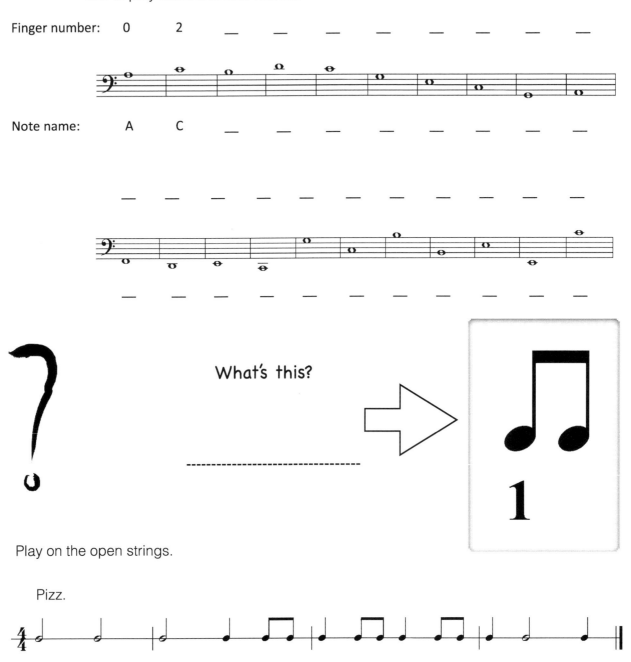

Play on the open strings.

Pizz.

The next piece uses only the open strings of the cello.

```
Listen to this piece:
5. Open strings cello
  The mp3 files that accompany this book are available
at http://www.arts2science.com.
```

Open Strings

Moderato — Carla Louro

3
The First Position

In this chapter, you will be introduced to the first position. You will learn about key signatures, fingering charts, scales, arpeggios, rhythm exercises, popular pieces and
preparatory exercises for the pieces. Many exercises will encompass the four strings, so you will have a good knowledge of the positions and finger numbers in all strings.

This chapter pays particular attention to rhythm, teaching you the quarter notes, half notes, whole notes, eighth notes and many others, ending with exercises and pieces. You can also find important information on technique and theory that appears in small boxes that resemble notes that a student would take during a cello lesson.

There are also improvisation exercises and revision charts with all the notes in the first Position.

Good Work

The First Position

First Position: C Major

There are finger positions for your left hand when you play the cello. The positions tell you where to put your fingers to play the notes. In each position you won't move your left hand when you play on different strings.

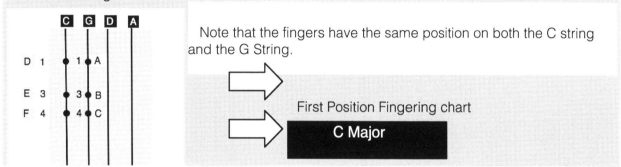

Note that the fingers have the same position on both the C string and the G String.

First Position Fingering chart

C Major

Remember how to write the notes from the C Major scale in the bass clef.

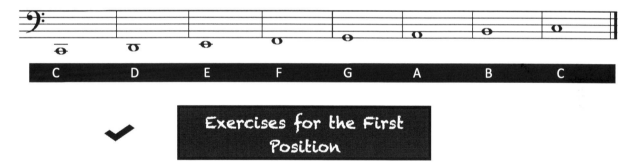

Exercises for the First Position

Find the note names and finger numbers that are missing.

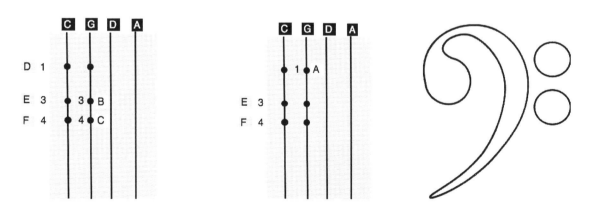

Play the interactive application to learn about the first position in the folder that accompanies this book (with a virtual cello):

"The cello scales and the first position"

Play the next exercise in first position, in C Major.

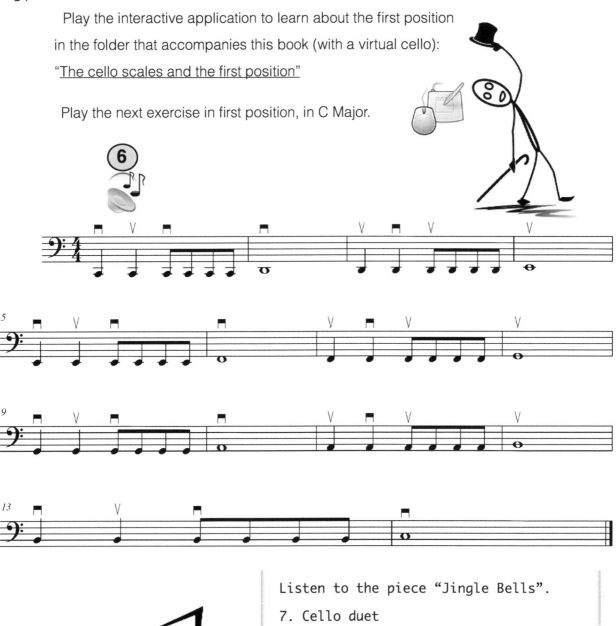

Listen to the piece "Jingle Bells".

7. Cello duet

Listen to the piece "Twinkle, twinkle little star" for cello duet.

8. Cello duet.

The mp3 files that accompany this book are available at

http://www.arts2science.com.

Play a Piece: cello duet

A duet is a piece for two instruments. In this duet you will play the second cello part. The first cello part can be played by your teacher or another cello student. The "Jingle Bells" theme is in the second cello part.

Jingle Bells

"Twinkle, Twinkle Little Star" is a well known English nursery rhyme. The lyrics come from a 19th century poem which is called "The Star" by Jane Taylor. The music is an english version of the original French folk song "Ah! vous dirai-je, Maman". This piece is based on the piano composition from the "Twelve Variations on Ah vous dirai-je, Maman" by W.A. Mozart, which are variations on the French tune. The student will play as Cello 1.

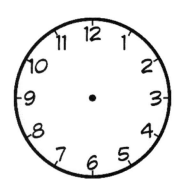

Twinkle, Twinkle Little Star

W.A. Mozart
arr. Carla Louro

Copyright©2011 Arts2Science All Rights Reserved
http://www.arts2science.com

Focus on Music Theory

Staccato	♩	When you play **Staccato**, you play short notes. Staccato is represented by a dot above or below the note.
Legato	♫	When you play **Legato**, you connect the notes without breaking the sound. Legato is represented by a slur between the notes.

Exercises for playing legato and staccato

Play the following exercises to practice staccato and legato techniques.

When you play staccato on the cello, you keep the bow on the string and make a pause between each staccato note that you play.

Play the next exercise, using the middle part of the bow.

Exercises for the First Position (continued)

Play this exercise in the first position.

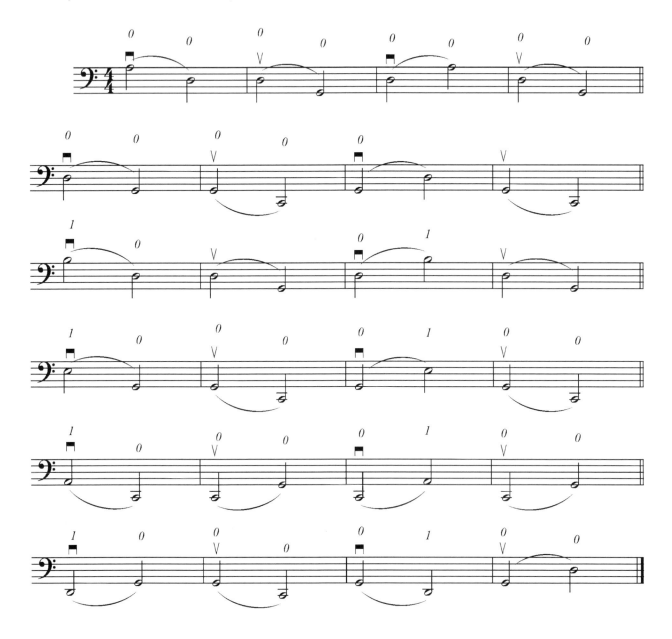

This exercise will help you practice the **management of the bow**.

T	F
Half bow, near the tip.	Half bow, near the frog.

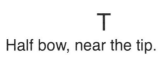

W
Whole bow

W during this exercise, you will always use the whole bow.

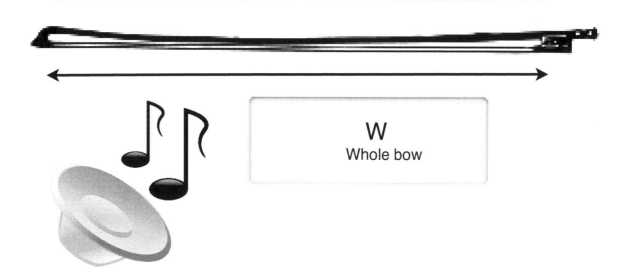

In this exercise you will practice using the entire length of the bow. You will also practice using only half the length of the bow.

Exercises for the Left Hand

KEEP FINGER IN PLACE

The exercise in the next page will encompass all the strings. This will help you achieve a good knowledge of the positions and finger numbers in all strings.

You will practice keeping one of the fingers of your left hand in place over one string, while playing on another string with the other fingers. This is a very important technique you need to master so you can play several musical pieces.

- For exercises 1, 2 and 3, keep finger 1 in place;
- For exercise 4, keep finger 2 in place;
- For exercises 5 and 6, keep finger 3 in place;
- For exercise 7, keep finger 2 in place;
- For exercises 8 and 9, keep finger 3 in place.

What will you do in the next exercise?

_____

_____

This symbol means that you should keep the finger in position until the end of the line.

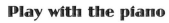

Play with the piano

A cellist plays many times with piano accompaniment. You will practice playing with the piano in the next piece.

Focus on Music Theory

Scales   What is a **Scale**? A Scale is a sequence of notes that appear on ascending or descending order. A Major Scale has two half steps: the first between the third and the fourth degree of the scale and the second between the seventh and the eighth degree of the scale. The other intervals are whole steps. An interval is the distance between two notes.

The diatonic scales have 7 different notes (degrees) and repeat the first one.

Look at the notes from the C Major scale, how they are ordered and how they are written for the cello:

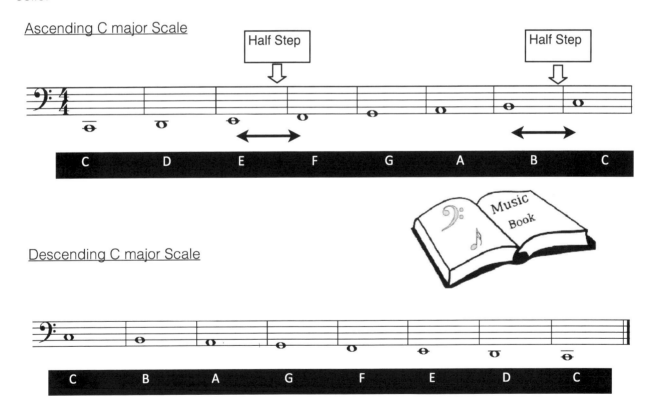

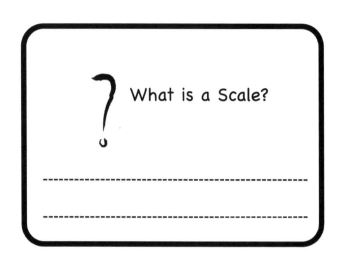

What is a Scale?

_____

_____

Play the C Major Scale

in one octave

Play the interactive application to learn about the C Major Scale in the folder that accompanies this book. There you can play an interactive cello: "The cello scales and the first position".

You can listen to the 4/4 drums rhythm accompaniment in the same folder to play with the scale. You can choose different speeds: 60, 80 and 120.

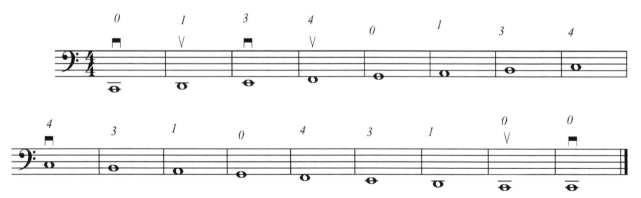

Half steps and **whole steps**. You play a half step with consecutive fingers and a whole step leaving one finger in the middle. For example, you will play a whole step with fingers 1 and 3, or 2 and 4.

Exercises for Half Steps and Whole Steps

Practice half steps and whole steps in the first position in C Major. Play them and watch the finger numbers. Find other half steps and whole steps.

Look at the fingers that you will use to play the C Major scale. Notice the half steps and the whole steps.

Whole step from C to D

Whole step from D to E

Half step from E to F

Whole step from F to G

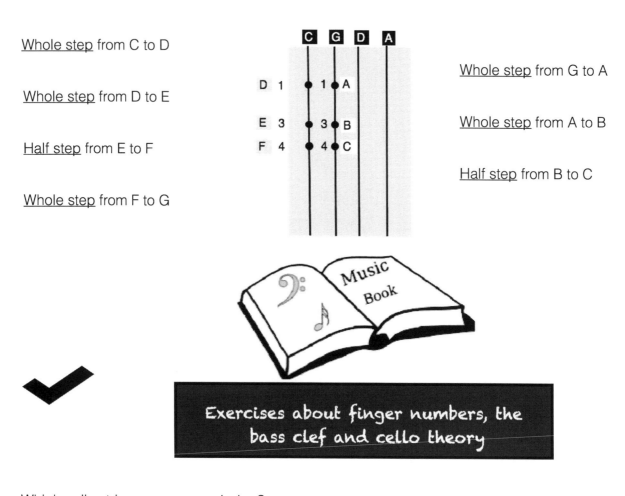

Whole step from G to A

Whole step from A to B

Half step from B to C

✓ Exercises about finger numbers, the bass clef and cello theory

Which cello string names are missing? _____

Draw the notes from the C Major scale and then write down the note names. Write down the numbers of the fingers in the boxes.

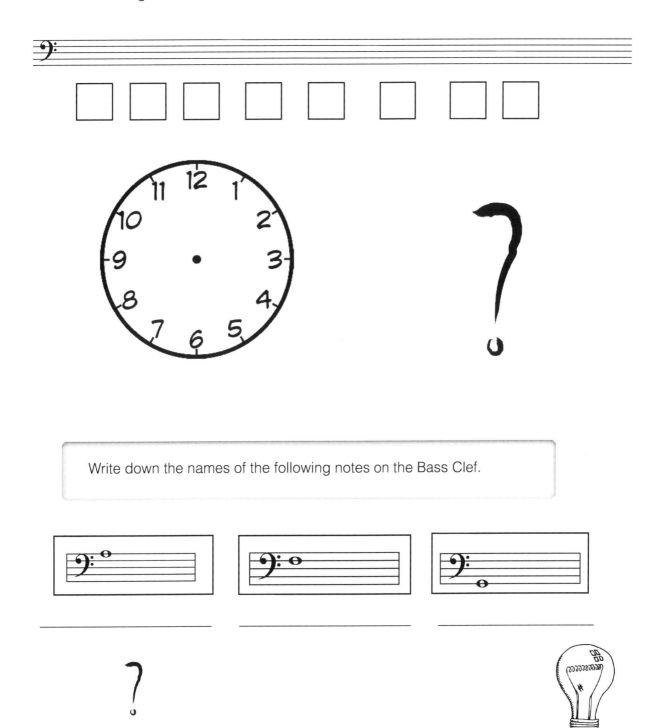

Write down the names of the following notes on the Bass Clef.

First Position G Major

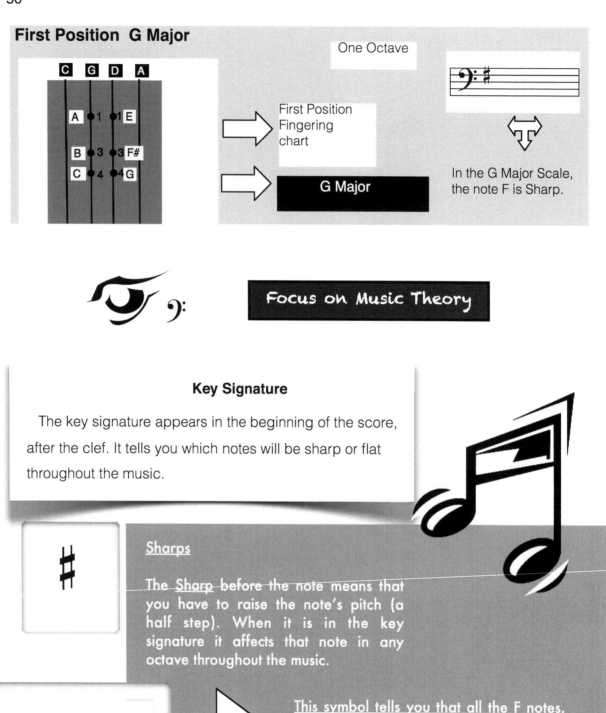

One Octave

First Position Fingering chart

G Major

In the G Major Scale, the note F is Sharp.

Focus on Music Theory

Key Signature

The key signature appears in the beginning of the score, after the clef. It tells you which notes will be sharp or flat throughout the music.

Sharps

The Sharp before the note means that you have to raise the note's pitch (a half step). When it is in the key signature it affects that note in any octave throughout the music.

This symbol tells you that all the F notes, in any octave, are sharp throughout the piece, unless a natural symbol appears before the note F.

Play the G Major Scale

SCALE IN ONE OCTAVE

 **15** You can use the "Bebop" rhythm accompaniment in the same folder to play with the scale. You can choose different speeds: 70 and 120.

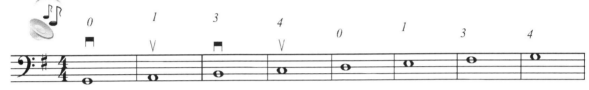

Which finger plays the F Sharp?

Play the interactive application to learn about the G Major Scale in the folder that accompanies this book. There you can play an interactive cello:
"The cello scales and the first position".

Exercises for the notes in G Major

Now you will see the note in the staff and you will write down which finger you will use and the names of the notes.

The notes in G Major.

Which note is sharp?
_____

Finger number: 0   1   ___   ___   ___   ___   ___   ___

Note name: G   A   ___   ___   ___   ___   ___   ___

Before you play the next piece, practice only the bow on open strings, so you will manage an even bow, without being affected by the left hand. It is very important for your sound to be able to maintain an even bow.

Practice only the bow on open strings. This will help you play the next piece with an even bow.

Lightly Row

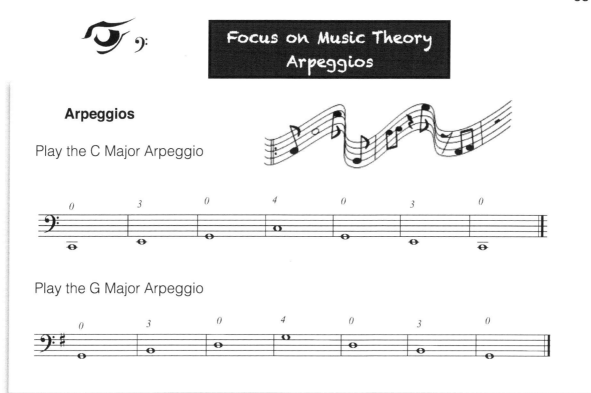

Focus on Music Theory — Arpeggios

Arpeggios

Play the C Major Arpeggio

Play the G Major Arpeggio

Exercises with arpeggios in first position

Practice arpeggios.

Focus on Rhythm

Note Duration

♫ 1	2 eighth notes — 1 beat	
𝄽 1	quarter note rest — 1 beat	
♬ 1	4 sixteenth notes — 1 beat	
♩. 1 2 3	dotted half note — 3 beats	

Exercises to practice rhythm

Practice the following rhythmic phrase on any string.

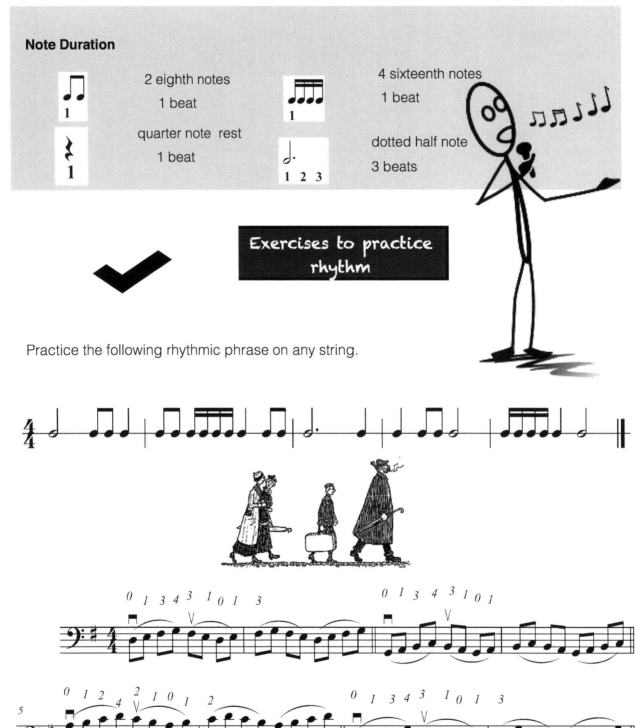

Focus on Music Theory

Natural Symbol	♮	The Natural symbol cancels the previous accidentals of a note, which are created by the sharp and the flat symbols.
Repeat Bar	:‖	The backward repeat bar tells you that you have to go back to the beginning of the piece or to the previous forward repeat bar. When the numbers **1.** and **2.** appear on top of the measure with the repeat symbol, you play the measure with **1.** the first time and the measure with **2.** the second time, not playing **1.**

Happy Birthday

Go Tell Aunt Rhody

American Traditional

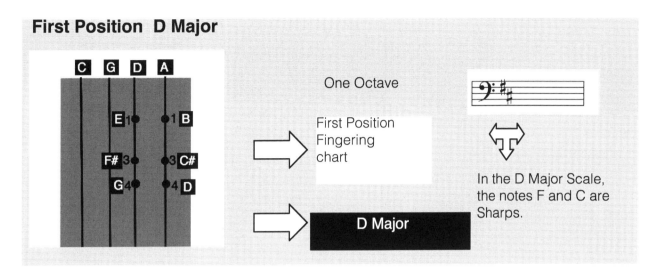

D Major Scale

D Major Arpeggio

Exercises for the D Major scale

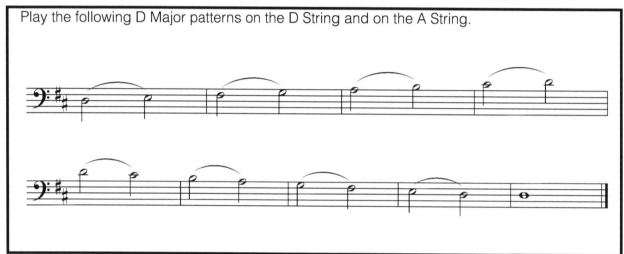

Play the following D Major patterns on the D String and on the A String.

Focus on Rhythm

Practice drawing dotted quarter notes and practice the rhythmic figure below.

Dotted quarter notes Play a dotted quarter note, followed by an eighth note.

New World Symphony

Dvoràk
arr. Carla Louro

CHRISTMAS SONG

IN D MAJOR

The First Noel

Christmas Song

Lyrics

The First Noel, the Angels did say
was to certain poor shepherds in fields as they lay.
In fields where they lay keeping their sheep
On a cold winter's night that was so deep.
Noel, Noel, Noel, Noel
Born is the King of Israel!

A **Round** is a musical form in which several instruments play the same melody, but don't start playing at the same time. The next piece can be performed by four different players. Each player enters according to the number that appears in the score. You also have a version of this piece written for violins, so they can play with the group as well.

Focus on Music Theory

Time Signature

The <u>Time signature</u> tells you how long each measure is. There are several types of time signatures.

In <u>Simple time</u> you have:

Duple Time	**Triple Time**	**Quadruple Time**
Two quarter note beats in a bar	Three quarter note beats in a bar	Four quarter note beats in a bar
2	3	4
4	4	4

 ### Exercises to practice rhythm

Practice the following rhythmic exercises on any string.

You can use the rhythm accompaniments in the folder that accompanies this book. You can choose different speeds.

Find the note names and the numbers of the fingers that are missing.

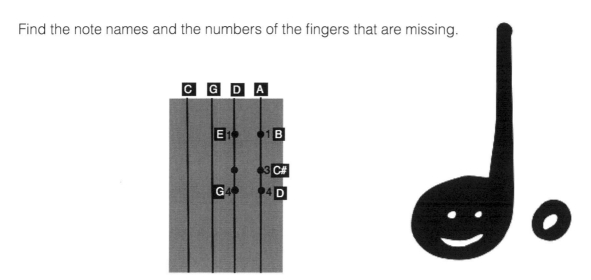

Choose the right option to complete each bar.

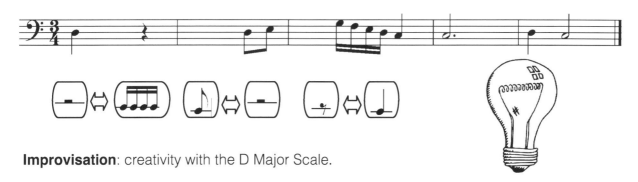

Improvisation: creativity with the D Major Scale.

Now you will use your own imagination and play a melody with the notes from the D Major Scale. You can write down the notes that you played. You can use the following notes:

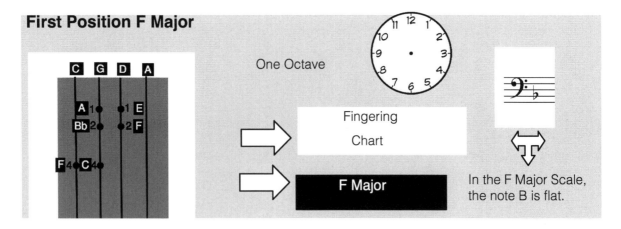

F Major Scale

F Major Arpeggio

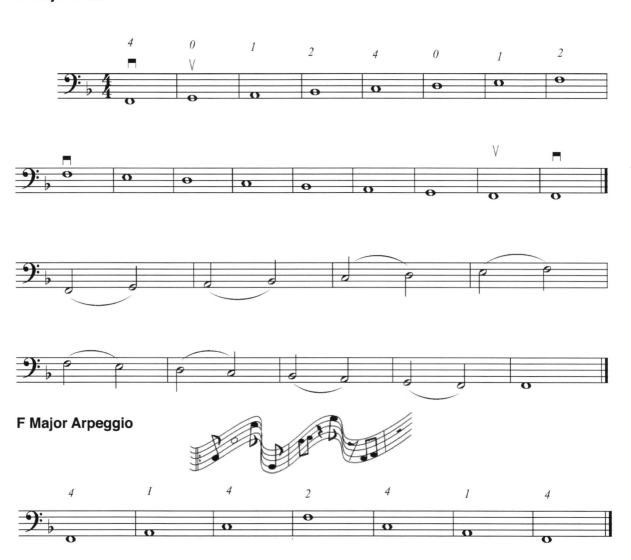

Focus on Rhythm

Rests Rests are symbols that show how much time of silence is in the music. Each symbol shows the length of the rest.

	Whole note rest 4 beats		Quarter note rest 1 beat		Sixteenth note rest 1/4 beat
	Half note rest 2 beats		Eighth note rest 1/2 beat		Eighth note triplets 1 beat

Triplets Eighth note triplets are 3 eighth notes that are to be played in one beat, instead of the normal 2 eighth notes in one beat.

WHAT'S THIS?

Listen to this melody.

Minuet 2

Johann Sebastian Bach

Focus on Rhythm

Dotted quarter notes

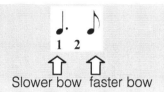

Revision

Slower bow   faster bow

 Exercises for the management of the bow and music theory

Practice different bow lengths. When you play the dotted quarter note, move the bow slower. When you play the eighth note, move the bow faster.

Down bow again

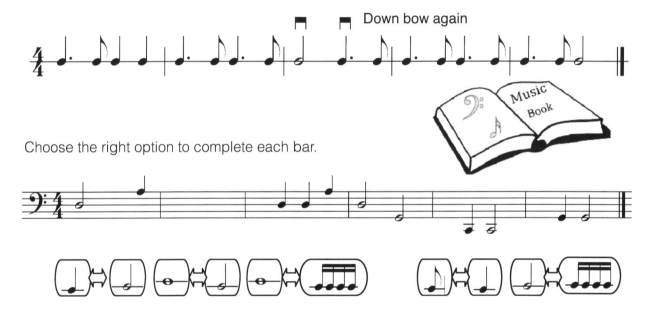

Choose the right option to complete each bar.

Some of the finger numbers are missing. Write down which fingers will play the notes.

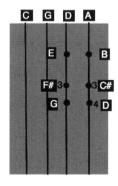

First Position extensions: D Minor

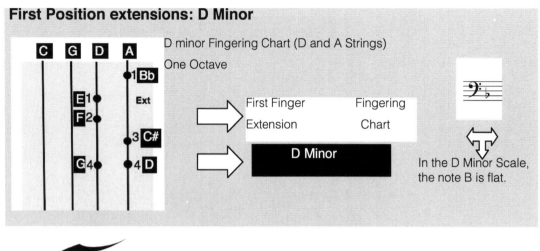

Minor scales : Natural, Harmonic, Melodic

There are three kinds of minor scales: natural, harmonic and melodic. The A minor natural scale has the notes A B C D E F G A. All the notes are natural, like in the C Major scale, but starting in the note A.

The **A minor harmonic scale** is the same as the natural minor, but we raise the seventh note of the scale (note G in the A minor scale). For example, in the A minor key, the harmonic minor scale is:

The **A minor melodic scale** is different from the other two minor scales: you play the ascending scale raising the sixth and seventh notes of the scale and you play the descending scale like the natural scale, without raising any note.

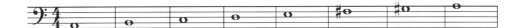

In the D minor harmonic scale:

1. Which finger will play the B flat?

2. Which finger will play the C sharp?

1.--

2.--

D MINOR HARMONIC SCALE

72

In this book you will be playing harmonic minor scales.

D Minor Harmonic Scale

D Minor Arpeggio

Minor Scale

Moderato   Carla Louro

> This <u>canon</u> can be performed by only one player or by eight players, playing the same melody at different times. You also have a version of this canon written for violins, so they can play with the group as well.

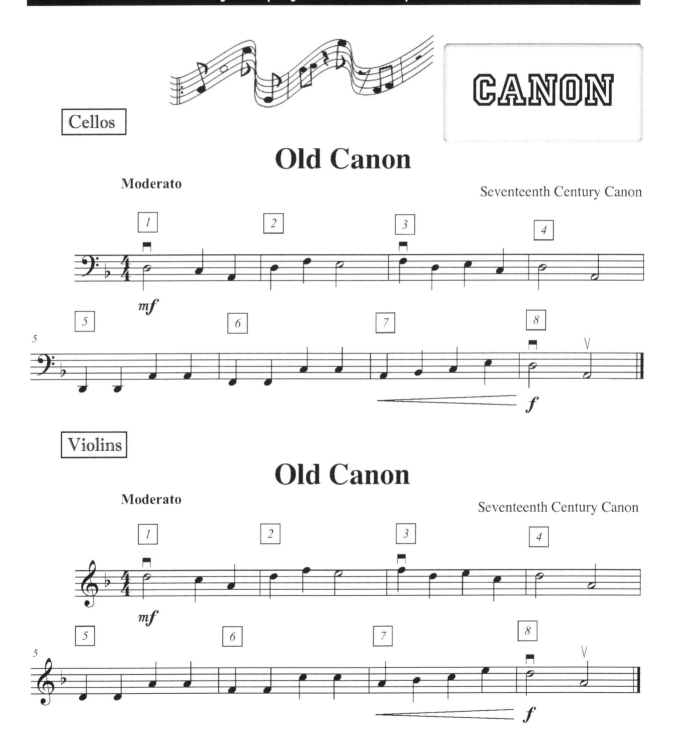

First position extensions: G Minor

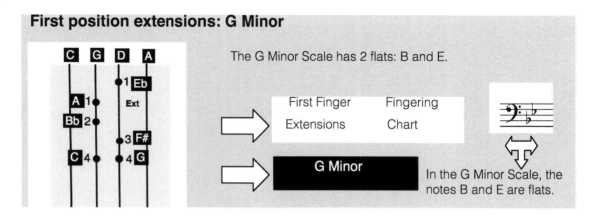

G Minor harmonic Scale

G Minor Arpeggio

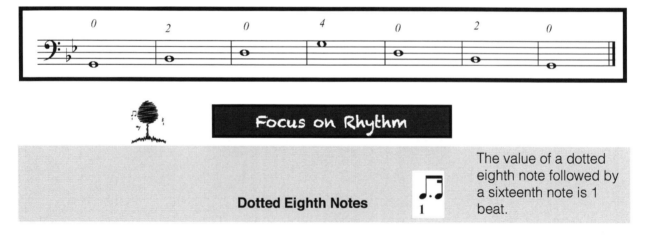

Focus on Rhythm

Dotted Eighth Notes — The value of a dotted eighth note followed by a sixteenth note is 1 beat.

Play the following rhythmic phrase on any string.

Dynamics

We speak of *dynamics* when we want to express how loud or soft a sound is. There are several symbols to express this:

- *p*   piano is an italian word for a soft sound.
- *mp*   mezzo piano is louder than p.
- *mf*   mezzo forte is louder than mp.
- *f*   forte is an italian word for a loud sound.

Não se me dá que vindimem

Portuguese Traditional

Wie komm ich denn zur Tur herein

J. Brahms

76

In the next piece, you will play as cello 1.

Focus on Music Theory

Tie	A Tie is a curved line that connects two notes that have the same pitch. It means that you should play them as a single note, with a duration that is the sum of the two notes. Note that the Tie is very similar to the Slur.
Slur	When you see the Slur between the notes you play the notes in one bow. The next musical theme has Ties and Slurs.

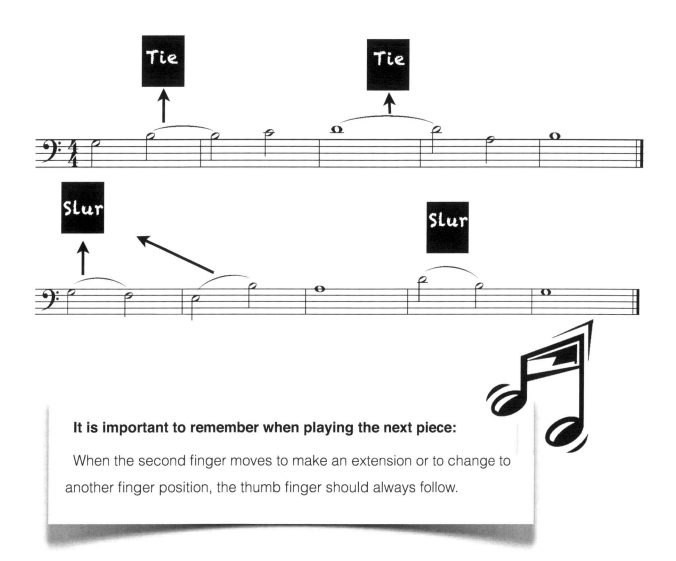

It is important to remember when playing the next piece:

When the second finger moves to make an extension or to change to another finger position, the thumb finger should always follow.

Page 102: piano accompaniment.

Senhora do Almurtão

Traditional Portuguese from Beira Baixa
Arrangement by Carla Louro

First position extensions: D Major

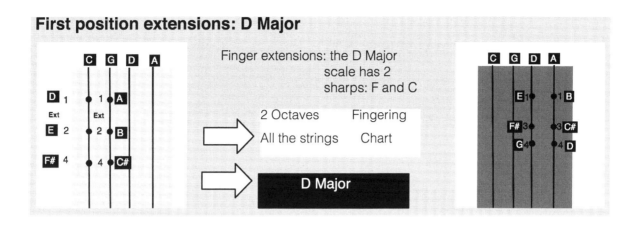

SCALE IN TWO OCTAVES
AND ARPEGGIO

Lyrics (extract) from "Mary had a little lamb":

Mary had a little lamb,
Little lamb, little lamb,
Mary had a little lamb,
Its fleece was white as snow.

And everywhere that Mary went,
Mary went, Mary went,
Everywhere that Mary went
The lamb was sure to go.

"Yankee Doodle" is a well-known Anglo-American song.

It is from the time of the Seven Years's War.

Yankee Doodle

American Song

Spring
The Four Seasons

Allegro

Antonio Vivaldi

First position extensions: A Major

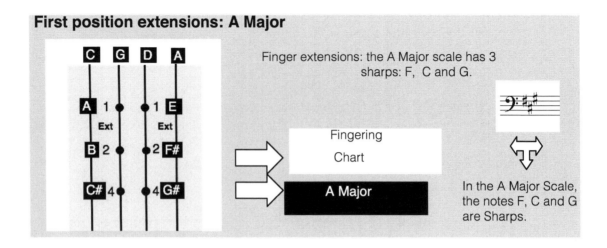

A Major Scale: 1 octave.

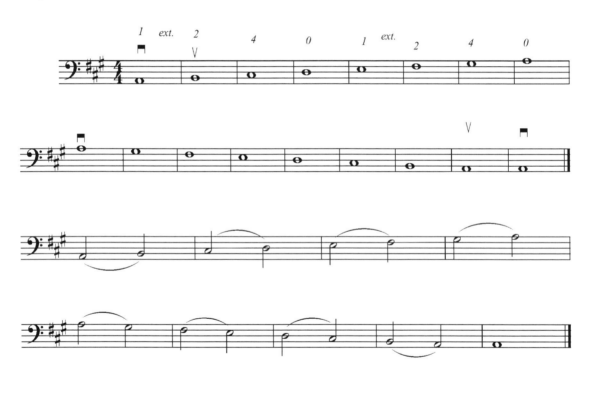

A Major Arpeggio: 1 octave.

Exercises for pieces in A Major

Play this exercise on the other strings as well.

William Tell is an opera composed by Gioachino Rossini, an Italian composer of many operas. He was born in 1792 and died in 1868. He also composed the famous opera "The Barber of Seville".

William Tell

Gioachino Rossini

Focus on Music Theory

Transposition Sometimes a music piece changes from one scale to another.

When we transpose a melody, we play the same melody starting on a different note.

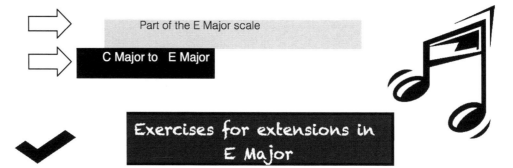

Part of the E Major scale

C Major to E Major

Exercises for extensions in E Major

Transposition from C Major to E Major

The piece "Morning Song" by Grieg starts with a melody in the C Major Scale and then the melody is transposed to E Major.

Morning Song

Page 100: piano accompaniment.

Edward Grieg
arr. Carla Louro

Extract from Étude nº 1 from 113 Violoncello-Etuden by Dotzauer

ÉTUDE BY DOTZAUER

First Position Revision

Before you learn another cello position, take a moment to review the first position.

Play some of the previous pieces again if you need it.

First position revision piece: "Scarborough Fair"- english traditional theme.

Lyrics:

Are you going to Scarborough Fair?
Parsley, sage, rosemary and thyme

Remember me to one who lives there
She once was a true love of mine.

4
Repertoire pieces and different music styles

This chapter will introduce you to improvisation and music styles, such as blues. It also includes a list of several scales and arpeggios.

You can also look for other resources to work further on the rhythm and theory concepts that you've practiced throughout the book. You can go to the www.arts2science.com website and use the free cello theory and exercise applications and sibelius scorch files. There are also additional pieces and exercises for you to download.

You can also go to the http://www.solfege.org website, where you can download the GNU Solfege application, which is an ear training program written to help you train intervals, chords, scales and rhythms. It is a free software and is part of the GNU Project. The program is intended to help music students with their ear training. It is available for many platforms and in many different languages.

You can use only this book, or you can use it with other books as well. There are two very useful cello method books that you can use, both for the beginner and the intermediate level. These books are:

- a beginner and intermediate method book: "Méthode du Jeune Violoncelliste" by L.R. Feuillard, published by Edition Delrieu;
- a book with cello exercises, also for the beginner and intermediate level: "113 Violoncello-Etuden, Book 1" by Dotzauer, published by Edition Peters.

Focus on Music Theory
Double Stops and Changing meter

Double Stops   Playing double stops is playing two strings of the cello at the same time.

Changing meter   When you play the piece "Folk Song" on page 94, you will see that the meter will change many times from duple time to triple time. Try to play only the rhythm before you play the notes.

Exercise Double Stops

Focus on Music Theory
Music Styles, Blues

Blues Scale Blues is a music style that has its origin in the African-American communities of the United States. It comes from spirituals and work songs from the 19th century. The six note blues scale (like the A Blues scale that we are going to play) has six notes that come from the minor pentatonic scale, plus the raised fourth degree.

A Blues Scale (your teacher can play this scale for you).

Exercises for Blues and double stops

Play this double stop exercise in Blues Style.

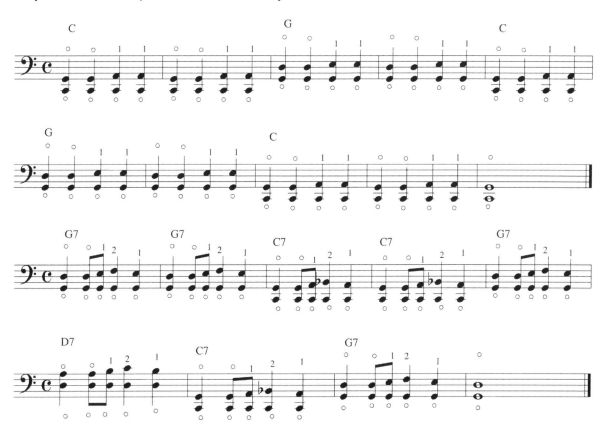

Blues in G

Carla Louro

Blues in G

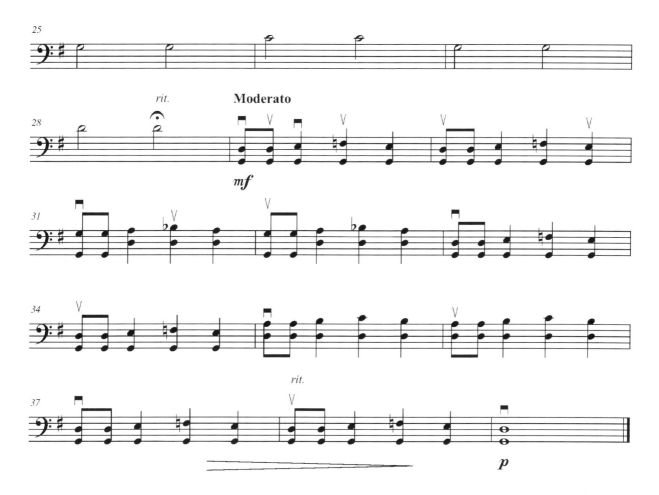

Page 106: piano accompaniment.

Folk Song

Carla Louro

Scales and Arpeggios in two octaves

Major Scales: Two Octaves (in first position).

You can play these scales with different rhythms:

C Major Scale and Arpeggio

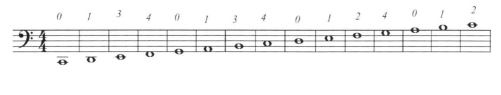

D Major Scale and Arpeggio

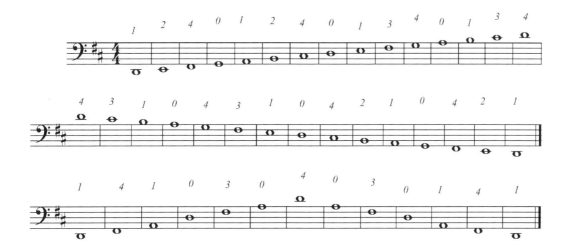

Here you have different patterns for some scales.

D Major scale: one octave

D minor scale: one octave

G minor scale: one octave

D Major scale: two octaves

5. Piano Accompaniments

Ode To Joy

Beethoven
arr. Carla Louro

Copyright©2011 Arts2Science All Rights Reserved
http://www.arts2science.com

We Wish you a Merry Christmas

Christmas Song
arr. Carla Louro

Eine kleine Nachtmusik

Wolfgang A. Mozart
arr. Carla Louro

Morning Song

Edward Grieg
arr. Carla Louro

Copyright©2011 by Arts2Science All Rights Reserved
http://www.arts2science.com

Morning song

Senhora do Almurtão

Moderato
♩ = 90

Traditional Portuguese from Beira Baixa
Arrangement by Carla Louro

Senhora do Almurtão

Senhora do Almurtão

Senhora do Almurtão

Folk Song

Carla Louro

Folk Song

Printed in Great Britain
by Amazon.co.uk, Ltd.,
Marston Gate.